Advance Praise for
AUTISM AND HOLY ORDERS

Thirty years ago, St. John Paul II outlined four "pillars" that are essential in a seminarian's preparation for the ministry and life of a priest: human, spiritual, intellectual, and pastoral formation. He intentionally began with human formation for the following reason: "The whole work of priestly formation would be deprived of its necessary foundation if it lacked a suitable human formation" (Apostolic Exhortation, *Pastores Dabo Vobis*, 43). Deacon Sutton applies this key concern of JP II as it pertains to assisting seminarians with autism, a developmental disorder that may be overlooked or misunderstood. I have consulted with Deacon Sutton on human formation issues for more than 10 years, and I have seen his insights applied in concrete situations. Vocation directors, seminary formators, and bishops will appreciate his professional and practical insights. I highly recommend *Autism and Holy Orders*.

—*Most Rev. Mark L. Bartchak,*
Bishop of Altoona-Johnstown

Dr. Sutton has done a tremendous service to all who minister in religious formation and to the Church at large. Every vocation is a gift from God and, now more than ever, dare not be squandered. This book masterfully identifies autism not as an insurmountable barrier to a genuine vocation, but as a condition that can in most cases be easily managed for the benefit of the person, his religious community, and the Church.

— *Archabbot Martin Bartel,*
St. Vincent Archabbey, Latrobe, Pennsylvania

AUTISM and HOLY ORDERS

How to help seminarians with autism become effective priests

by Deacon Lawrence R. Sutton, Ph.D.

Foreword by Scott Hahn

PITTSBURGH:
Lambing Press, 2022

Copyright 2022 by Lawrence R. Sutton.

Other books by Lawrence R. Sutton:

Teaching Students with Autism in a Catholic Setting (Loyola Press)

How to Welcome, Include, and Catechize Children with Autism and Other Special Needs: A Parish-based Approach (Loyola Press)

Contents

Foreword	vii
1. Why this book is necessary	1
2. Autism and mentoring	7
3. Intellectual ability	23
4. Executive function and theory of mind	33
5. Communication and boundaries	45
6. Depression and anxiety	67
7. Rigid behaviors, stimming, and sensory sensitivity	75
8. Welcoming new seminarians (some of whom may have autism)	87
9. Pastoral year, transitional diaconate, and priesthood	93
10. In closing	99

Foreword

There is a certain mystique surrounding autism. Daily, it seems, the media bear news of another celebrity self-diagnosis. Actors and rock stars speak casually of being "on the spectrum." In academia, scholars apply the terms freely to historical figures who are long dead. Autism is used to explain someone's prodigious ability to focus—or utter inability to focus. The self-appointed experts multiply, and it is as if the public conversation is a replay of Genesis 11, with the Lord declaring once again: "Come, let us go down, and there confuse their language, that they may not understand one another's speech."

Meanwhile, the number of actual diagnoses steadily rises, and marketers try to exploit the situation by hanging products on the label—drugs, dietary fads, and special supplements.

The word is everywhere, and yet the over-exposure doesn't help anything. In fact, it seems an impediment to real understanding. The confusion grows.

But then a book like this arrives and offers great hope.

Dr. Sutton is a real expert in the field of autism. A licensed psychologist, he served the Commonwealth of Pennsylvania as regional manager of its Bureau of Autism Services. An ordained deacon, he is now director of pre-theology formation at St. Vincent College and Seminary in Latrobe, Pennsylvania. He has written two well-regarded books on teaching and catechizing students with autism in a Catholic setting. He has traveled the world to train educators in the methods he developed.

The man has spent a long career preparing to write this book—a book that needs to be read by many Catholics.

I have been waiting for decades for such a book to appear. I have taught men in pre-ordination formation at several seminaries and universities, in the United States and in Rome, and I have seen far too many men suffer needlessly because of misunderstanding of their condition.

In these pages, Dr. Sutton writes with clarity and concision. He knows there is an urgent need to bring order to the conversation—for the sake of the Church and for the sake of clergymen and seminarians with autism.

Autism and Holy Orders will be useful for faculty and formators, bishops and abbots. But my hope is that it will gain a much wider audience. It should be read by parents of boys and men with autism who are considering the seminary. It will be useful to the candidates themselves, for their own self-understanding and for their experience of community life. It can be tremendously helpful for parishioners who wish to understand the priests with autism who serve them.

I rank many such men among my best students, and I have seen them excel in pastoral roles. The trials they have suffered give them insight into others' problems.

God calls each of us—all of us—as we are. Think about the prophets of the Old Testament and the apostles of the New. They had their challenges, and they acknowledged them. Isaiah confessed that he was woefully inadequate to the task God had assigned him.

Guess what: It didn't matter. God supplied the means of formation and the necessary opportunities for growth, and he still does this today. Dr. Sutton identifies these elements and gives excellent counsel for making the most of them, especially mentorship.

I believe, very strongly, that this book will be a great and providential opportunity for many men in the years to come. Thanks to Lawrence Sutton, we can now begin a truly informed conversation about autism and holy orders.

Scott Hahn
March 7, 2022

1. Why this book is necessary

I'm a practicing clinical psychologist and a deacon in the Catholic Church. I managed the Western Office of the Pennsylvania Bureau of Autism Services, and for the past nine years I have worked at St. Vincent Seminary in Latrobe, Pennsylvania. In all of my professional capacities, as well as in my service as a deacon, I have worked with many people who have autism spectrum disorders.

Every year, my seminary has three or four men with some form of autism. In addition, I know priests and deacons who I am sure have the disorder, although it may never have been suspected, diagnosed, or treated. In addition to being strong Catholics, these men are often very intelligent and highly motivated to become good priests. They have mastered the intellectual rigors of college and passed initial psychological evaluations for entry into the seminary.

They may, because of their disorder and where they fall on the autism spectrum, have trouble with certain social aspects of life and the priesthood—but managing their issues is often straightforward and uncomplicated. A bishop or abbot might consider these straightforward, uncomplicated solutions simply "common sense"—something the man should be able to take care of by himself—but the seminarian, priest, or deacon with autism may need help in order to recognize both the problem and the solution.

It's common for a bishop or abbot to have a man in formation who has a few behaviors that are so odd, so irritating, that the situation seems hopeless. The man has to *know* how he seems to others, doesn't he? So those counterproductive behaviors must be intentional, or else the result of extreme arrogance, right? This book asks that bishop or abbot to reconsider whether the man may have autism, and may have the makings of a good priest if his disorder is diagnosed by a psychologist familiar with autism, who initiates specific mentoring practices both before and after ordination.

My hope is that several audiences find this book helpful. The primary audience is bishops and abbots (and parents and friends) of seminarians and priests with an autism spectrum disorder. I want this book to offer them hope, mentoring ideas, and perhaps a new perspective on autism. I present brief case descriptions of many seminarians and priests I have worked with over nine years. The descriptions include both their strengths and their mentoring needs within the four dimensions of religious formation: human, spiritual, intellectual, and pastoral. I also discuss my insights about these men's ability to work independently as priests and pastors in a diocese or religious community.

The second group that I hope will find this book helpful is men who have autism—or who think they *may* have autism—and who believe they are called by God to holy orders. Whether these men are seminarians, priests, or deacons, I hope this book will encourage them to visit a psychologist and learn what is creating obstacles between them and their calling. If the diagnosis is indeed autism, I pray that these men will find a bishop or abbot willing to understand, or at least to value the seminarian enough to learn more, and that the methods of mentorship I describe in this book will help them.

And finally, I hope this book can help parishioners who have a priest or deacon (or friend or loved one) with autism. It is a complex disorder that often can be managed very simply. Just understanding why people with autism act the way they do is a big step toward being able to communicate with them effectively, enhancing your life, their life, and life in the parish or monastery.

Every diocese and seminary has—or should have—a clinical psychologist on staff or on call to determine whether autism is an issue for a seminarian. This is not arrogance on my part: unless a clinician has had specific training about the autism spectrum and how to diagnose it, attempts at diagnosis will often fail. A developmental or clinical psychologist can point out ways in which non-psychologists can guide men with autism through seminary and create an atmosphere that will support these men's unique gifts, allowing them to be productive, healthy priests. Many psychologists today have such training.

If you stop reading right now, let this be your takeaway: men who may have autism often need only two types of intervention in order to flourish. They need a diagnosis by a clinician knowledgeable about autism, and they need mentoring by willing peers, instructors, superiors, a spiritual director, and a formator, who "get" autism. Diagnosis and then mentoring: that's what this book is about.

We desperately need more well-formed, happy priests. If a man feels called to be a priest, it only makes sense to do what we can to help him through seminary and into a strong, productive priesthood.

At the Sea of Galilee, Jesus called unruly, hot-headed, impetuous Simon to become a "fisher of men." It's hard for us to understand what Jesus was thinking, placing his greatest trust in this man who was so obviously *not* pastoral material. Yet with God's help, Simon Peter became the man God called him to be.

It's the same for men with autism. With God's help (and some compassionate, knowledgeable mentoring), they can become the priests God is calling them to be: the priests the world needs.

To protect their privacy, I have changed the name of every person whose story I have used for illustration in this book.

2. Autism and mentoring

A *developmental disorder*, by definition, is one that becomes noticeable in early childhood. It is usually permanent. Common developmental disorders include vision and hearing impairments, physical impairments, and intellectual impairments.

Depending on the particular developmental disorder, it may be treatable with medication, therapy, or other methods to decrease the disorder's effects —in other words, it may be *managed*—but a developmental disorder will never be *cured*. The person with any developmental disorder will have it for a lifetime. Management is the key.

Autism is a complex disorder, and scientists aren't sure what causes it. (For brevity, this book will often use the term *autism* for *autism spectrum disorder*.) According to the National Institutes of Health, possible causes are genetic mutations, interactions between genes and the environment, or a biological factor. One thing is certain: autism is not rare. It has greatly increased in prevalence over the past several decades. The Centers for Disease Control and Prevention state that in 2020, about one in every forty-four eight-year-old children was affected by autism, and boys were more than four times more likely to have autism than girls were.

Given these statistics, it's not surprising that out of all the men called to serve God as priests, some will have a high-functioning form of autism.

In these pages, I'll occasionally mention children with autism. I won't dwell on children, because my aim is to help adults (regardless of whether they were diagnosed and treated as children). But understanding how the specific autism behaviors of an adult began in early childhood is critical in learning how to help that man in adulthood.

Notice the name: autism disorder occurs on a broad *spectrum*. Some men with autism may have little or no expressive language and limited intellectual abilities. These men will likely not finish high school in a traditional sense and will never make it into a seminary. Others may be extremely intelligent, or gifted in one or more areas, or may have disabilities that become apparent only occasionally or in specific situations. These are the men who, if they feel called by God to become a priest, will make it into seminary and are as likely to be good priests as any other seminarians.

To enter seminary formation requires high intelligence. A man must be capable of reading and understanding undergraduate-level philosophy, graduate-level theology, and foreign languages. Many of the men I reference in this work are in fact gifted and superior in intelligence. They generally performed extremely well academically and had a good use of verbal language.

Autism is not a mental illness or a psychiatric disorder. It does not signify spiritual weakness or a flawed character. In fact, the reality of living with the hardships of a developmental disorder can create deeply spiritual men of exceptional character. Most people with autism do not need medication, psychotherapy, or psychiatric treatment. They simply need help learning to manage aspects of their lives.

Professionally diagnosing autism spectrum disorder

Professional diagnosis—at any age—is the critical first step in helping someone who has autism. Psychologists diagnose autism by observing a person's behavior and development during early childhood. Common signs include poor social skills, limited or confused communication, repetitive behaviors, and a limited range of social interest and activities from birth to age five.

The optimal situation, of course, is for parents to notice things about their child's behavior and development as early as possible, take their child to a psychologist, get a diagnosis, and then learn the best ways to teach and communicate with their child. For many reasons, this early diagnosis and treatment is not always possible or simply doesn't happen.

The good news is that doing a *thorough developmental history*, even in adulthood, can go a long way towards helping someone with undiagnosed or untreated autism. A developmental history uses the memories of a caregiver from when the adult with possible autism was an infant and toddler. A parent or caregiver who has known the person from birth or early childhood is the best source of this history. There are other good methods, but they're considered secondary to someone who can provide solid first-hand developmental information.

Why is it necessary to get a thorough developmental history of a young man entering seminary formation? If the man has a good academic standing, good references from his family and parish priest, and no pre-existing legal or background issues, why would a psychologist want a long, detailed early-life history? The answer: Not every adult with autism has been *diagnosed* with autism. Once identified, the disorder can be managed—and the earlier the seminary clinician identifies the disorder, the better for the seminarian, the seminary, and the diocese. Most behavioral idiosyncrasies can be modified and managed (not eliminated) before ordination if they're addressed when the man first enters the seminary.

Seminarians who are undiagnosed

When a man arrives at the seminary with a diagnosis of autism, the clinician should be informed so that he or she can help the new seminarian from the outset. Most adults with autism, however, have never been diagnosed. The seminary needs a process for seeking a diagnosis when a seminarian is having difficulty, and the clinician should play a critical role in that process.

Here's how it works at St. Vincent Seminary: The rector, academic dean, or one of the faculty members approaches me and explains a problem that he or she is having with a seminarian. Then I meet with that seminarian about the problem. If, after a conversation with him, I suspect autism, I get his permission to seek a detailed developmental history and may perform other tests.

After I've identified the seminarian's issues, which may include possible autism, I get to know him a little. Then I meet with the rector's council and the faculty to explain the man's learning style and nuances. This helps the seminarian and faculty coordinate purposes and perspectives.

Think of it like this: A seminarian with an alcohol problem will attend regular support meetings to manage his sobriety. A seminarian with medical needs will take prescription medication. A seminarian with a disability may need assistive technology or classroom accommodations. And a seminarian with autism needs just a few people who understand his form of autism and can help him manage his behaviors on the journey towards becoming an excellent priest—the goal of everyone involved.

I cannot stress this enough: The seminary's psychologist must be the one to request and then interpret a seminarian's developmental history. As with any complex medical diagnosis, non-specialists should never attempt to diagnose autism. *What-*

ever the diagnosis, it will affect the entire future of that man, so it's important to get it right and then manage it correctly.

Being shown how to manage his autism will increase the seminarian's experiences and education at seminary, his effectiveness in the world, his quality of life, and the quality of life of those around him. Seminarians and priests with autism have clearly shown the intellectual capabilities necessary for priesthood: after all, they successfully performed through high school and college and into seminary. What they need more than anything else is compassionate, informed mentoring. The more intelligent the man, the more successful the mentoring will be.

Alex

My biggest surprise in my first year working at St. Vincent Seminary was meeting Alex, a bright seminarian and a very complicated man. He was a loner, didn't have a best friend or even an ongoing relationship with a peer, and had never dated.

- He tended to overthink everything.
- Every time he made a comment and someone reacted differently than he expected, he chas-

tised himself for not anticipating that reaction from them.

- He couldn't sit still in the classroom, and he blurted out answers, often before the professor finished asking the question. Needless to say, professors found this highly irritating.

- At times, bored by material that he had read in advance, Alex had trouble staying awake in the classroom. Worse, he also had trouble staying awake during monastic prayer. This became so severe that he was evaluated for a sleep disorder; the results were negative.

- When he didn't get his way immediately, or if he misinterpreted someone's intentions, Alex would rage loudly in his bedroom.

Finally, the rector recommended that he come to me for help controlling his temper. Alex had never been diagnosed with autism, but was nonetheless sure that he was autistic. He was willing to send home a developmental history questionnaire to his parents. From the results, I learned two things: his uncle had been diagnosed with autism, and Alex himself had a preponderance of symptoms, as a toddler, that would have supported a diagnosis of high-functioning autism.

As an adult, Alex's autism manifested itself in difficulty knowing how to quickly read and respond to the emotions of others. When he couldn't do this, he would blow up. In session, we practiced more acceptable ways to *express* his frustration. (He usually was unable to talk about situations immediately after they happened.) We also developed methods to *relieve* his frustration, including some sort of physical exercise. Walking wasn't physical enough, running was good, and chopping wood was amazingly successful.

A breakthrough happened that first winter. I was about to leave for the weekend and Alex was rapidly pacing in my office, clearly agitated. My suggestion: "When you find yourself really upset, go outside and wash your face in the snow." (My thinking was that he needed something to disrupt the anger process.) When I saw him on Monday, Alex greeted me with a huge smile and a bear hug, saying, "It worked!" He had washed his face with snow, and it had startled him so much that his anger stopped. Alex had the skill set to manage his anger once he was settled to a certain point; this simple exercise demonstrated that to him.

Never having dated, Alex found women fascinating but didn't know how to approach them. Being near any woman he found attractive usually caused him to blush bright red—which was going to be a problem in the future when women approached him, as a priest, for counseling. I enlisted the cooperation of a willing female college student, and Alex practiced with her how to do basic socialization with women. Later in formation he became a chaplain for one of the female sports teams. This all desensitized him, in a slow, purposeful way, to being around women.

Alex's *diagnosis* could have been done only by a clinical psychologist who understood autism and recognized some of the more subtle symptoms. In addition, only a clinical psychologist should request the detailed developmental history from parents. However, most of the *mentoring* Alex needed could be performed by anyone, even a willing peer, with a little guidance from me.

Recognizing that Alex might have an autism spectrum disorder early in his seminary studies gave me six years to explore possible problem areas before they became unmanageable. Today, Fr. Alex is an exceptional homilist who makes scripture so real to his congregation that it's easy to forget he's a young, recently ordained priest.

Samuel

A child named Samuel illustrates how we can never be sure what another person knows or doesn't know. (This is true of everyone, of course, whether or not they have autism.) Soon after I was ordained a deacon, I met a family with a toddler—I'll call him Samuel—who had been diagnosed with an autism spectrum disorder. When I first met Samuel, he didn't say any understandable words, he didn't seem to be able to follow direction from his parents, and his attention span was only a few seconds. Later, in elementary school, it became apparent that he was very good at imitating his peers. That was when I first thought of including him as an altar server.

When he was not quite fifteen, Samuel had been helping the sacristan for two years. I arrived early one day for a special Eucharistic service and found everything ready: fresh linen on the altar, priest vestments opened and set out, candles lit, programs on each chair—everything in order before any priest, deacon, or sacristan had arrived. Samuel had done it all, learning the details just by observing.

Mentoring to provide real alternatives

Mentoring someone with autism means recognizing what the person with autism needs to do and helping him find a way to do it as independently as possible. Almost any issue can benefit from mentoring, and a mentor can often be anyone. The very best outcome is when the mentor is no longer needed, at least for that particular issue.

With Alex (above) I used *direct mentoring* (although I also worked with him as a counselor). The two of us role-played and practiced repeatedly how to react in certain situations. We did this so that if the situation reoccurred—and it likely would—he would have a *real alternative* to choose from. A real alternative is more than just an intellectual understanding: it's something that the person has practiced alone or with a mentor, or even performed in real life, so that he knows it's not only possible but also effective in that situation. (I've learned that when someone goes into a rage and does not have a real alternative, he will likely do what he always has done in the past, even if he knows intellectually that there are better alternative behaviors.) Alex and I discussed actions that effectively interrupted his anger long enough for his intellect to take over—and then we practiced them; that was direct mentoring. When he washed his face with snow after my impulsive suggestion, it was nothing we had practiced—but it worked. It was a breakthrough because it gave him a real alternative behavior that he knows, from experience, will be effective.

Samuel's case involved *indirect mentoring*. He simply watched the sacristan, priest, and deacon closely and then mirrored their behavior. He knew whom to watch, he was motivated to do well, and he learned his responsibilities perfectly. There was no stress involved, and he had time to watch and learn calmly.

Observation and practice, role-play and practice

Learning new skill sets often requires either observation and practice or role-play and practice. In my two-semester pastoral counseling classes, we read and discuss concepts and theories and then the seminarians practice on real people (non-seminarian students acting out various roles). All seminarians—with and without autism—observe how their peers handle the interviews and also how I direct or redirect the interviews. The purpose of this course is to expose seminarians to pastoral counseling problem-solving. They could read about it all day long, but the only way to really learn how to solve problems is to be put in situations where they must solve problems, and to be helped through those problems if they need it.

An ordinary whom I regard highly once stated that he understood how it made sense to pair a seminarian or new priest who has autism with a good, seasoned priest from whom he could learn how to be a good priest—but because the mentor priest could never be with the new priest in the confessional, how could we teach the sacrament of Reconciliation? (Again, that question could apply to *any* seminarian, not just one with autism.)

My answer to that ordinary was to describe our method. We start with practice confession sessions using role-playing volunteers. Then a mentor priest and classmate seminarians critique the sessions and provide feedback.

No newly ordained priest is fully prepared. Is *any* newly ordained priest the best possible confessor? It takes practice—and much of this practice is possible *before ordination*.

SUMMARY

Chapter 2: Autism and mentoring

- Developmental disorders are behaviors that become noticeable in early childhood. The disorders are permanent. They cannot be cured but can often be managed.

- Autism spectrum disorder (autism) is a developmental disorder with a broad spectrum of traits and intelligence. The symptoms vary from person to person.

- Autism is not a mental illness, a psychiatric illness, a lack of intelligence, a spiritual deficit, or a character flaw.

- A psychologist must be the one, as part of the initial evaluation, to request and interpret a developmental history of the seminarian who shows signs of possible autism.

- A real alternative behavior is one that has been practiced so that it comes naturally in a given situation.

- For seminarians or priests with autism, mentoring often provides the best help.

3. Intellectual ability

A child born with autism is atypical—has a developmental disorder—*but is not necessarily intellectually impaired.* Recognizing this is essential to understanding autism. A person with autism may have lower-than-average functioning in some areas and average or even above-average functioning in other areas. In 2009, the Royal Society published a paper finding that as many as one in ten people with autism appear to be remarkably gifted in various skill areas.

The difficulty in ascertaining true intellectual ability in people with autism causes much heartache and frustration for parents and others. They may think, "If he can talk about cars in such detail, why doesn't he talk to me when I ask him a question? If he can multiply five-digit numbers in his head, why doesn't he respond when his mother hugs him?"

A man who has made it through college and entered the seminary may be assumed to have the high level of intelligence necessary for the priesthood. Many people with autism, however, need to be explicitly taught the skills that other people develop effortlessly. A man with autism can learn to compensate for his skill deficits, often by carefully following scripted behaviors and modeling his peers and mentors. This, however, requires focused and intentional intervention by a knowledgeable mentor, formator, or spiritual director.

People with autism typically learn easily by watching others. The higher the functioning level of the person with autism, the better he will be at learning by watching and at developing "scripts" about how to act appropriately in a given situation.

The bishop, abbot, or seminary professor needs to recognize that despite the high intellectual abilities a student may have, he may need—for instance—step-by-step instructions when he's introduced to a subject that he has no experience with. Once he receives the simplistic-seeming instructions, the seminarian will ordinarily pick up the new subject quickly and will no longer require direct help on that subject.

Greg

Greg's testing experiences illustrate beautifully how difficult it is to know the intellectual level of someone with autism. When he was five years old, Greg had a measured I.Q. (intelligence quotient) of 64, which is in the range of mild intellectual impairment. Greg had relatively good expressive language, did not have notable behavioral problems, and attended a typical kindergarten. He was "invisible" in school—for example, he did not volunteer answers to classroom questions—but he would answer when called on, and did his work, for the most part, with no disruptive behaviors.

When Greg turned eighteen, his intelligence quotient was measured again to see if he met the requirements to receive Social Security Disability entitlements. Greg's I.Q. at that time was 72.

At age twenty-one, Greg finished his secondary education (high school). He was approached by the Office of Vocational Rehabilitation (a federal program which every state uses, often under a different name) to see if he would consider being evaluated for vocational interest, job identification and training, and intellect. Greg's I.Q. was tested for a third time, and he achieved a score of 94, which is in the average range of intelligence – two standard deviations above his first score.

All three of these tests, and all three I.Q. results—of 64, 72, and 94—were considered valid at the time of testing and are still considered valid.

I.Q. scores commonly vary by a few points over the years, but intelligence itself never makes huge leaps. Greg's intelligence didn't increase by a whopping thirty I.Q. points. He was probably always in the average range of intelligence. Here's what most likely happened: Over the years, he developed the ability to understand and process information more quickly and efficiently, which led to higher testing scores.

Anthony

Anthony was not a seminarian, but was interested in the Church and in religion. I first got to know him professionally as my patient and, later, in an adaptive religious education program.

His early development was slower than that of other children his age. As an infant and toddler, he didn't look at or towards his mother very often. As a young child, he didn't respond to verbal cues. He didn't say his first words until he was nearly nine years old.

He was his parents' first child, and didn't have much contact with other children his age. It took Anthony's parents a while to realize that something wasn't right with their son. Because of his lack of language and responsiveness, his parents took him to an audiologist when he was about two; his hearing was not impaired. Then they took him to a speech and language pathologist. Soon after, Anthony was referred to me, and I diagnosed autism.

Because Anthony didn't talk or use any form of expressive language, he was often misunderstood and would express his frustration by injuring himself. For instance, he would bang his head on the floor or table and scream. Sometimes he would strike his face with a closed fist. The blows didn't seem to hurt him; he appeared to have a high tolerance for pain.

When Anthony finally began communicating verbally at nine years of age, he always responded slowly. When someone asked him a question, he would sometimes need one to two minutes to answer. His answers were usually correct, but often the other person, frustrated from waiting so long, walked away before hearing the answer—or worse, answered for Anthony or talked over him before he could fully respond.

With his language impairment, Anthony couldn't take standardized intelligence tests or achievement tests in school. His teachers thought his intelligence was low, and tried to steer him into a life-skills curriculum to learn basic daily living skills. His parents, however, insisted that Anthony receive as normal an education as possible.

When he was fourteen, Anthony enrolled in my parish's autism religious education program. His faith mentor was a bright high school freshman girl. In an early class, she asked Anthony if he ever received the sacraments of Reconciliation and the Eucharist. Anthony responded, "Do you mean confession?" and then quickly added, "Do you mean like Cain and Abel?" To the astonishment of his father and me, Anthony then proceeded in a slow, smooth, methodical way to tell the story of Cain and Abel.

I had been Anthony's psychologist for ten years, and this was the first time I had heard him say more than a few consecutive words. His father had no idea how Anthony knew the story of Cain and Abel; neither he nor Anthony's mother had ever told him the story. Up to that point, Anthony had never participated in a parish religious education program or even attended Mass. None of us had any idea how a boy who was thought to have a significant intellectual disability could seemingly pull this story out of thin air and express it so clearly and correctly. The trigger seemed to be his young mentor's question about the sacrament of Reconciliation. It could also have been that the mentor, a girl his age, was giving him undivided and focused attention, to which he responded positively.

Anthony received the sacrament of Confirmation when he was twenty. Over the course of his six years of religious education, he learned about the gifts of the Holy Spirit and was able to explain them and, to some extent, say what it meant to be an adult in the Catholic Church. At the time of his Confirmation, he was able to recite common prayers and was participating in some small-group activities, even though he still preferred to spend time by himself. He attends Mass each week and appears to understand the rituals. He receives the Eucharist regularly, and is now an active, involved member of his parish.

My experience with Anthony reminded me of several important communication behaviors that I need to use consistently with people who have autism.

- I need to express my thoughts fully, using complete sentences.
- I need to explain things clearly and completely, even if I receive no feedback from the other person indicating that he has understood or even heard what I said.

Eye contact and evidence of listening are rare from people with autism, but that doesn't mean they're not listening and understanding.

A note about speech-reading

Eye contact is difficult for many people with autism because eyes often convey either very subtle or very strong meanings and emotions. Even people *without* autism can misinterpret looks from another person; for people *with* autism, the difficulty is much greater, and many manage this difficulty by simply not looking people in the eye. The problem is that when people talk to a professional, such as a priest, they expect the professional to make eye contact; outright avoidance of the eyes is not an effective management technique. To the other person, it can feel rude or dismissive.

As a young psychologist, I worked at what is now called the DePaul School for Hearing and Speech. We taught the children to speech-read (read lips). Although I was never as proficient as the Sisters of Charity and other teachers, I did learn to speech-read. In my work, I've found that speech-reading can be a valuable skill for many people with autism. I try to teach seminarians and priests with autism simple speech-reading techniques.

Learning these techniques can solve a number of problems. The person with autism can avoid the other person's eyes, but that person won't be offended, because the person with autism will still be focusing on the face (specifically, the lips). It will be obvious that the person with autism is listening actively and with interest. In addition, the person with autism will receive the information in two complementary ways.

SUMMARY

Chapter 3: Intellectual ability

- People with autism are atypical in that they have a life-long developmental disorder, but are not necessarily intellectually impaired. They may be brilliant in some aspects of life and have high intelligence, yet need mentoring in other areas.

- The I.Q. of someone with autism is often hard to measure, even for skilled clinicians, because his information processing abilities improve as he ages.
- A man who has made it through high school and college and entered the seminary may be assumed to have sufficient intelligence to complete seminary and become a capable priest.

4. Executive function and theory of mind

Autism can reveal itself in many ways. Two broad, common areas of impairment in people with autism are *executive function* and *theory of mind*. Together, they're responsible for many, if not most, of the difficulties people with autism face.

The good news is that both executive function deficits and theory of mind deficits respond well to the right kind of intervention and mentoring.

Executive function

Executive function concerns the area of the brain that controls the ability to manage cognitive processes such as memory, attention, problem solving, organization, reasoning, and language. These skills allow us to accomplish things and generally move forward in life. Executive function allows us to think abstractly, adapt to change, and anticipate what might occur in the future. To a greater or lesser extent, many people with autism have impaired executive function.

Because it controls so many important activities, impaired executive function can manifest in a number of ways. For example, many people with autism have difficulty understanding cause and effect. They don't recognize that something they do in one moment may affect later events. This makes it difficult for them to make plans or organize tasks. Many people with autism also seem to have difficulty generalizing from one learned concept to a similar learned concept, or understanding how the same concept can be applied to different situations.

Is impaired executive function a deal-breaker for a man who feels called to be a priest? The answer is a resounding NO. The reality is that *these skills can be taught and learned*. Remembering things, finding the best way to problem-solve, getting organized, learning to listen well and speak effectively: This is all teachable and learnable. There are many methods and aids to help anyone—with or without autism—become stronger in all of these skills.

(And for what it's worth, there appears to be a strong correlation between high intelligence and impaired executive function. Think of the archetypal "absent-minded professor" who does brilliant work but is never quite sure what day it is.)

Here's one example of impaired executive function. Even a gifted seminarian with autism may have trouble *getting started* on a paper, assignment, or project. He will need specific instructions on how to begin. (See Chapter 5.) Many men with autism don't ask for help because of their own expectations. They may believe that they should be able to remember what to do without an aid (for instance, a calendar, a peer reminding them, or notes from class) because they didn't need such aids in college. Often, they avoid asking for help because they believe that their peers have no trouble getting started on their own; it would be embarrassing to stand out by admitting they need help getting started.

This is where mentoring is especially beneficial. A mentor—who could be a peer—can help by simply having a conversation about ways to choose a topic, begin research, or write an outline, opening paragraph, or first draft.

Although it may seem elementary, one of the most valuable tools for a seminarian or priest with autism is a large written or pictorial schedule in his room showing day, week, and month. Being able to see what comes next without having to worry about keeping the information in their head is even more useful to people with autism than it is to people without autism. Here's how this schedule might look:

5:15—5:45	Shower and dress
5:45—6:00	Organize books for the day
6:00—7:00	Holy Hour in the chapel
7:00—7:15	Morning prayer in the chapel
7:15—7:45	Mass in the chapel
7:45—8:30	Breakfast in cafeteria
8:30—9:15	Modern Church History, room 104 Brownfield Center

For a seminarian with autism, this simple schedule provides clarity and reduces the anxiety about possibly forgetting. Simple pocket notebooks are easy to carry and use. They are popular with many students, whether or not they have autism, and are essential for some. If the seminarian uses a pocket notebook to jot down assignment dates and details and then puts that information on the larger calendar in his office, computer, or room, it's just one more simple tool in managing his own executive function issues.

Here are some other ways to help men with autism learn to strengthen their executive function skills.

- Pair the seminarian with an upperclassman as a major source of information about classes, schedules, how things are done at the seminary, the "unspoken rules," and other helpful information that the seminarian with autism might not learn on his own. (See Chapter 8.)

- Encourage the seminarian to make a friend in each class with whom he can compare class notes, review and clarify assignments, and study for tests.

- Encourage the seminarian (if necessary, *help* the seminarian) to ask for testing accommodations if they're needed. Accommodations might include additional time to take the test, a quiet room, or oral testing. The purpose of the test shouldn't be speed, the ability to tune out ambient noise, or the ability to write; the test should show whether the seminarian has understood the material and integrated it into his overall formation.

- Help the seminarian identify a "liturgy peer" to model: an upperclassman who performs difficult liturgical tasks correctly and in a fluid, effortless-looking way. (The upperclassman doesn't need to know that he's been identified as a "model.") Watching this person performing his job will show the seminarian with autism what well-performed liturgy looks and sounds like.

- Make sure that the seminarian has both a spiritual director and a human formator who understand autism. The visible "odd" behaviors associated with autism are most likely forms of communication when the seminarian doesn't understand something or has more stress than he can manage. The spiritual director and the human formator can help the seminarian learn how to respond better.

These suggestions would be helpful to *all* new seminarians, but they're crucial for seminarians with autism.

Theory of mind

Theory of mind is the psychological term for the understanding that other people have beliefs, desires, attitudes, and feelings that are not necessarily the same as one's own. (It is a theory because the mind isn't directly observable.) A newborn doesn't grasp that his mother's mind is separate from his; all he knows are his own wants and needs. Children without autism or other related disorders gradually learn, as they grow and develop, that what is in other people's minds is separate from and sometimes different from what is in their own minds. Then they begin to sense what someone else is thinking or feeling, and observe evidence that their sense was correct or incorrect.

Theory of mind is the basis for empathy. We can't have intimate relationships without it—and it is often impaired in people with autism. It gets in the way of making close friendships, and is the source of what seems—from others' perspective—to be self-centeredness.

Andrew

One Saturday, Andrew was sitting in the gym with several of his peers and they became engrossed in a heated discussion on a nuance of moral theology. Andrew, who was a self-proclaimed expert in moral theology even though he was very early in his seminary studies, jumped up from the group, ran to the exit, and left, slamming the door behind him. His peers were stunned. Five minutes later, Andrew returned, took his seat among his peers with a bright smile and a happy demeanor, and presented as if nothing had occurred—which further confused his peers.

When I asked him about the incident, Andrew explained that as a teenager, he'd had an explosive temper and would break things. He eventually went to a counselor who taught him to "slam doors" when he was upset. Andrew said that he had become upset in the discussion with his peers, got up, and slammed the door, which helped him regain control of his anger. He had then rejoined the group as if nothing had happened because *he* felt better, and had assumed that everyone understood what he had done and why.

I had trouble persuading him that there was a problem, but I did my best to explain that what he did as a teenager might not be sufficient or appropriate as an adult—particularly as a priest. We talked about other, better ways he could express his anger now, as an adult. Then we practiced those replacement behaviors over and over to make them real alternatives in the future.

Walt

In social situations, imitation is a frequent coping strategy of people with autism. Beginning in early childhood and continuing into adulthood, imitating others is usually a safe way to learn to fit in, but it's only a partial solution at best. It doesn't explain *why* others behave as they do, what social rules exist, or why those rules exist. Imitation without understanding can lead to humiliating situations.

I observed an embarrassing theory of mind misunderstanding following a baptism. Walt, a man with autism, watched carefully as family members came up to the mother of the newly baptized child and greeted her with hugs and kisses. Walt was not part of the mother's immediate family and had never met her. Nonetheless, he approached her, attempted to kiss and hug her—and was shocked when she pushed him away. He had made a mistake in guessing that hugging and kissing the baby's mother was something that *everyone* should do at a baptism. The "script" he observed was correct for some, but not for all.

Jack

Jack's case is the opposite of Walt's. We intentionally introduced imitation in order to help Jack socially. When he entered the seminary, he was very rigid in his mannerisms and gestures, particularly as he genuflected and presented for prayer and liturgy. He looked to others almost like one of the toy soldiers in *The Nutcracker*. He was unaware that his stiffness and rigid precision made him the focus of other people's attention and was a distraction, at times, from the liturgy or prayer.

He and I talked about finding an upperclassman role model, and settled on two men for him to observe and try to imitate as they smoothly entered the chapel, genuflected, knelt, and began praying. In this instance, Jack did not need to talk with or directly interact with these upperclassmen; he just needed to know who was considered a good model to imitate. Shortly after observing the two other seminarians, Jack's movements in the chapel became more fluid and he no longer stood out. His movements were still precise—they were still characteristic of Jack—but now he wasn't the focus as he had been before.

Lee

I didn't work with Lee, a bright man earning a doctorate who was employed privately for a number of years before entering the seminary. Lee was quiet and respectful, did well academically, seemed quite pastoral, and gave the impression that he would listen carefully for as long as necessary before offering guidance.

However, it became increasingly clear that if you asked him how he was, or how his family was, or what he thought of the weather, you'd get a detailed twenty-minute response. Because his peers and faculty didn't always have that much available time, to end a conversation with Lee they resorted to just walking away—but Lee would often turn from his own destination and walk with the other person to continue his side of the conversation.

He completely missed the social cues that it was time to end the conversation. He was one of the friendliest and most accommodating seminarians to graduate, and is a popular priest, but I hope he has someone working with him on this large issue. Often, people will say, "How are you, Father?" as a polite way to begin a conversation about their own needs and worries. I pray that he has learned to listen rather than to take the question as an invitation to focus on himself. (See the "Small talk" section of Chapter 5.)

To help a seminarian with impaired executive function issues or theory of mind deficits, mentoring is critical.

SUMMARY

Chapter 4: Executive function and theory of mind

- Executive function in the brain controls memory, attention, problem solving, planning, organizing, reasoning, and language.

- Theory of mind is the understanding that other people have beliefs, desires, attitudes, and feelings that are not necessarily the same as one's own.

- People with autism often have impaired executive function or theory of mind.

- Mentoring is a powerful way to help develop and strengthen executive function and theory of mind skills.

5. Communication and boundaries

("Communication" is a broad category covering many areas of life where people with autism may have difficulty. This chapter discusses general communication issues, literalness and gullibility, small talk, and social boundaries—especially boundaries with women. It also offers a useful checklist for seminarians to use when asking for help.)

Human communication is complicated even for people without autism. Effective, mature communication includes both verbal and nonverbal language—some of which is the same across our entire species and some of which varies by locality, family, profession, or individual. Rules for social interactions change depending on many factors, and people with autism often don't learn these rules just by watching others.

Delayed and impaired language development is a characteristic of autism. Some people with autism *never* develop functional language; that is, they never fully understand others and can never clearly express themselves well enough to have their needs met. Some people with autism have limited vocabularies. Even those with high-functioning forms of autism, who are capable of complex speech, may show abnormalities such as echolalia (repeating words spoken by others), unconventional word use, unusual inflection, speaking in a monotone, and mumbling or repeating to themselves what someone else has said before responding.

As I discussed in Chapter 3, some people with autism have difficulty with eye contact. Emotions coming through the eyes are often so subtle and yet, paradoxically, so strong and personal that the message is hard for a person with autism to understand. They find it easier to just not make eye contact. In addition, nonverbal communication cues such as body language, gestures, and facial expressions are subtle and often unreadable by someone with autism.

Autism seems to affect the brain's ability to process information. Sometimes sensory data gets jumbled, or the person's ability to understand language is impaired under certain kinds of stress. Common stressors include being excited or upset, being presented with a new situation, or feeling pressured to provide a spontaneous or immediate response.

The inability to understand subtle cues is particularly a problem when the person with autism is talking about a topic of interest to himself. He might go on and on without realizing that the other person has given clear signs of boredom. One teen with autism that I knew read obsessively about the prophet Isaiah and could recite from memory precise details. If no one intervened, he would talk about specific verses until he expressed every detail he had in his brain.

In a new situation for which he doesn't know the "script," a seminarian with autism will typically try to respond, but his response may miss the mark. Sometimes these errors will be minor and humorous, but sometimes, especially with boundary issues, people may think, "As smart as this guy is, he really should know better!" It's essential that a formator do a careful debriefing after each such incident. Find out exactly what happened and in what order, what the seminarian was thinking, and what he was trying to convey with his response.

If the situation requires it, administer appropriate consequences, but work with the man to make sure he understands how he went wrong and how to prevent it from happening again. This means not just *telling* him what a more acceptable response would be but *practicing* that response—that replacement behavior—to provide a real alternative (see Chapter 2).

To people with autism, it may seem that everyone around them can read minds, because we can apparently read faces, body language, gestures, and nuances of tone. Imagine what life is like for someone who can't do this. They'll talk happily about their favorite topic long past the point at which a polite listener has communicated in a dozen nonverbal ways that it's time to move on to something else. They may laugh at a funeral, not get a joke, or misunderstand friendly kidding. They may blurt out a remark about the way another person looks. They may often recognize that an emotion is called for but not know *which* emotion.

Literalness and gullibility

People with autism may not be able to sense when they're being lied to. I once worked with a teen with autism in a juvenile prison. He had been so eager to have a friend, and so focused on pleasing his friend, that he had done exactly what his "friend" asked him to do: commit a crime. When the police arrived, everyone else ran away and this young man stood there, puzzled.

William

Literalness and gullibility are issues for many people with autism. William was a seminarian who appeared to understand everything said to him—but he understood literally, in a concrete sense. He was also naïve, believing as literal everything said to him. Of course, this meant that he misinterpreted any friendly teasing from people who genuinely liked him. It also made him an easy mark for bullies throughout high school and college and even, I'm sad to say, in the seminary.

William spent many hours in session working on issues of depression and anxiety relating to his lack of self-esteem—which grew from his difficulty understanding other people's real intentions.

Through basic therapy, he became confident enough to *ask* people about the meaning of their interactions: to ask, first, his more trusted formators and seminarian peers, and later others. Gradually, his self-confidence grew enough that more aspects of his personality became visible and he was a happier man and priest upon ordination.

Small talk

Without mentoring or conscious modeling, a person with autism who finds himself in an unfamiliar situation or with unfamiliar people will typically either hang back and limit his interactions, or try to take over the conversation. People with autism often do not naturally understand how to initiate and engage in the social back-and-forth exchanges known as "small talk."

Small talk may seem simple and shallow, but in reality it is deep and complex, an important social code. Small talk is the secret password, the shibboleth. If you do it well, no one notices. If you do it poorly, some people jump to all sorts of conclusions about your intelligence and character. Instead of an undeveloped social skill, it becomes a moral issue to some people. Small talk is not for getting or

COMMUNICATION AND BOUNDARIES 51

giving information; it's just the lubricant in the social engine—but as the lubricant, it's critical.

One seminarian (now ordained) had no clue about small talk and always responded to questions literally. If someone asked, in passing, "How are you?" he would provide an explicit, literal description of everything going on in his life, including all of his medical, academic, social, and family concerns. He didn't understand that brief greetings such as "How are things going?" and even "How's the family?" are almost always just small talk: social lubricant. The literal meaning of the words is beside the point, but giving the expected answer is very important: "Great. And you?" Period—unless the initiator asks for more information.

Most of us have learned this effortlessly, watching others make small talk since we were children, but people with autism take things literally. They may need help understanding when small talk is the most appropriate response and when something broader or deeper is required. For example, suppose a seminarian is with his counselor and the counselor asks, "How are things going?" That situation is not the time for the seminarian to make small talk —it's the time for him to go deep. On the other hand, when the seminarian is ordained and becomes the counselor, and his counselee, at the beginning of the session, politely asks him how he is, a warm "I'm great, thank you" is the most appropriate response, briefly answering politeness with politeness. After that, the priest needs to be quiet and invite the counselee to talk about his or her issues.

This is simply common sense for many people —but don't we all know someone *without* autism who won't let anyone else get a word in edgewise? The only way such a person has a prayer of changing is for someone to kindly—perhaps privately— ask him to let others speak. It's the same when the person has autism. Someone needs to gently and respectfully point out where he goes wrong and suggest a better way to respond to people, a way that will have better social results. It may be as simple as showing the seminarian how to rephrase a question or greeting as his response.

Social boundaries

People with autism often don't naturally or automatically recognize social rules or boundaries, especially in new situations. For example, in attempting to communicate clearly, they may seem mean or disrespectful. (Often they are simply giving brutally honest feedback, without wasting time on niceties or having any awareness of the feelings of others.) A wise ordinary will keep that in mind if, for example, he asks a man with autism to give his opinion about something. That ordinary will likely receive a clear, honest, complete response to his question—possibly with more bluntness and detail than he expects. A mentor can practice with the seminarian a better way of giving a truthful but brief answer.

People with autism may not have an innate understanding of "personal space" and may stand or sit closer to others than our particular North American culture approves of. Or they might not understand the importance of letting someone else finish speaking before they begin talking themselves. (Again, these two traits aren't limited to people with autism; we all know people *without* autism who stand too close and interrupt too frequently.) If no one helped explain boundaries to the man when he was a child, he may routinely cross boundary lines as an adult, even with his superiors, and then not understand why people are upset with him. With a mentor, the man can discover and practice better ways to interact with people.

Teaching social boundaries is possible. Although verbal explanations help in some cases, most people with autism learn better through role-play and hands-on practice. They need to see, hear, and sense what they should do. Successfully learning new boundaries needs to be more than an intellectual exercise. It must be practiced physically in order for a true alternative replacement behavior to become natural.

Social boundaries with women

Many of the men with autism who feel called to the priesthood have had few, if any, close relationships with anyone outside of their immediate family. They may never have had a close male friend. And many have never dated or had a romantic relationship. Once they're in the seminary (which may be attached to a co-ed college or university), dressed in cleric garb (which minimizes the need for them to "fit in"), some seminarians may find it easier to talk to others than it has ever been for them. This includes talking to women.

Being able to talk easily with others is an important skill for a priest, and a man who has never talked to women socially needs to learn those particular rules and boundaries. Without help, he won't know how to be socially correct or understand and recognize when he approaches or crosses a boundary until, in many cases, it's too late.

For instance, a high school or college boy with autism who has a crush on a girl might not be deterred when she says, "Go away." He might innocently approach her again the next day, because every day is a new day. He might, in fact, approach her over and over, not understanding that a firm rebuff means she is not interested in him at all and that he is, in fact, doing something that is socially taboo, against school rules, and possibly illegal, bordering on harassment or even stalking.

A seminary needs to be prepared to teach these social boundary skills to men who have never learned them. Even men without autism may have had limited interaction with women and few chances to practice social talk or being friendly and approachable while staying within appropriate verbal and physical social boundaries.

It might be argued that it's not the responsibility of a seminary to teach basic early heterosexual development and relationships to its seminarians. However, we're talking about a valuable commodity: intelligent, spiritual men who believe they've been called to holy orders and are willing to do the hard work. A little remedial training in this very basic, very important area of formation seems like a wise investment.

Understanding social relationships can be difficult for anyone, and romantic relationships are even more complex. A seminarian will most likely avoid asking questions about sex or love, fearing possible removal from the seminary—yet this is precisely the type of education that men with higher functioning forms of autism require if they are to be effective clerics to all of their parishioners in the future.

Here are four examples of how the lack of social skills with women interfered greatly with the man's formation.

- Each time Chad was near a certain young woman who worked on campus, he became mute and embarrassed. He blushed and literally shook in her presence. He found excuses to go to her workplace several times a week in attempts to see her and talk with her. Ultimately, Chad left the seminary.

- Robert, a forty-eight-year-old seminarian, befriended a teen volunteer who was accompanying a Special Olympics group on an outing. Not understanding the propriety or boundary issues, after he first met her at the outing, he then spoke at length with her on the bus ride back to our facility and then began communicating with her on social media. He told me that he thought the college would be an excellent place for the young woman to get her undergraduate degree once she graduated from high school, and said that he had offered to show her around the campus. Understandably, this behavior from a forty-eight-year-old man frightened the girl's parents. The seminarian did similar things with other women and was open and transparent about the interactions—so open and transparent that it worried his peers and superiors. He clearly had no intention of becoming romantically involved with any of these women, but was simply looking for female friends that he could talk to or connect with. He was completely unaware of how his actions looked to others. Robert eventually left the seminary.

- Ted, a new seminarian, attempted to befriend his professor, sending her personal notes and making inappropriate comments to her (inappropriate from any student to a professor, and especially inappropriate from a seminarian to anyone). He told her that he thought she was "beautiful," that she "dressed very well," and that she had "very good taste in clothing." He asked her if she would "consider sharing a meal with a seminarian." After much discernment with his spiritual director, formation director, and vocation director, Ted withdrew from the seminary.

- Justin was a bright, dynamic twenty-six-year-old. He discovered at seminary, for the first time in his life, the specialness of women. This led to his trying to discern whether he should pursue a vocation of marriage or the priesthood. He was undertaking the conflicting tasks of studying to be a priest while trying to understand romantic relationships for the first time in his life. This almost guaranteed failure. It was the "magic of the collar" which gave him confidence and allowed him to feel safe around women. Justin discovered that women had different perspectives on life than men and discussed things differently than men. Much to his surprise and, frankly, his dismay, he discovered that he really liked being with women. He eventually departed from seminary study.

For each of these men, formal counseling and possibly structured mentoring before they entered seminary might have supported their formation and produced a different end result. The Church might have gained some wonderful priests if, at an earlier point, friends or counselors of these men had explained boundaries and worked with them to modify their behavior.

Having or not having a romantic relationship before entering the seminary is not necessarily the critical issue. What is critical is the ability to be comfortable and appropriate around all parishioners and communicate easily (speaking and listening) with everyone, including women. A priest must have insight into his own needs and desires, and must understand boundaries and their meaning—and he should have all this *before ordination*. Yes, good priests improve over time, but a man who is ordained without understanding these basic social concepts and behaviors is sure to fail, and may unintentionally damage his parishioners during the process.

Teaching social boundaries to men who are long past the age when most men learn them is complicated, especially when the seminarian is fully engaged in formation, but it's possible—and absolutely necessary.

- The formation director, or at least one of the members of the rector's council working directly with the seminarian, should be a clinical psychologist who understands autism and psychosexual development.

- Seminarians with and without autism should encounter simulated real-life scenarios in pastoral counseling classes. These scenarios should involve properly prepared male and female actors of various ages from the college community at large.

- When necessary, involve members of the rector's council, the local parish, or other organizations to simulate real-life situations for the seminarian.

- If the seminary is attached to a co-ed school, seminarians should serve as chaplains for male and female sports. This will help them socialize in a highly supervised situation.

Asking for help

A man with autism who has made it into the seminary may have adapted and learned so well over time how to act like the crowd that others think he fully understands what is expected regarding an assignment or project. Not only does he not verbalize his confusion, he often automatically pretends to understand. He has learned this skill in order to fit in and avoid embarrassment.

His lack of executive function skills probably makes it hard for him to get started on any new project or focus on a beginning. *Completing* the project well, often masterfully, is not a problem: it's *getting started* that he may need help with. And, of course, his efforts to avoid embarrassment early on will lead to even greater embarrassment when, later, he needs to ask for help or risk not turning in the assignment.

Often, the instructor has not clearly and in detail expressed all expectations for the assignment, because most members of the class don't need that amount of detail. In addition, if a seminarian consistently scores well on exams taken from reading material, the instructor may assume that there is no impairment relative to doing projects or writing papers. This is a danger. The seminarian with autism may require help and practice in asking for assistance right from the beginning.

Thomas

Thomas is one of the brightest seminarians I have ever worked with, and is now a priest. One of his issues is that he has trouble understanding abstract concepts without help. In the past, he would not typically ask for help when he got stuck. Instead, he would become frustrated and angry, throw things around in his room, and obsess about how "stupid" he was. Thomas holds himself to the highest expectations, and felt that he should simply *know* how to do these simple tasks without asking for assistance.

The most straightforward way I found to help him was a series of four steps. (Note: Thomas' particular problem was in getting started, but these steps work well to ease the anxiety of asking for help with *any* issue.)

1. First, I asked Thomas to outline the problem on paper. This allowed him to "see" the problem, made it less vague and abstract, and made it obvious that it was solvable.

Most people with autism think concretely and have trouble with abstractions—but for *all* of us, when a problem seems insurmountable, it *becomes* abstract, bigger than life, and hard to think about. Outlining the problem on paper makes it concrete, something that can be seen at a glance and arranged in some kind of order. Mentoring seminarians to make "outline it on paper" their first step whenever they're stuck will help them in a broad range of situations.

2. As the second step, I asked Thomas to do something physical, such as jogging or chopping wood. Doing this seemed to "unfreeze" him and helped him move forward.

When we're angry at someone else or ourselves, that emotion often gets in the way of rational thought. Doing something physically strenuous helps a frustrated man blow off steam in a productive, non-destructive way. If it's possible, he should do something that produces a tangible product or reward for his efforts, such as chopping wood, vigorously cleaning up a storeroom, or painting walls. Afterward, he'll likely be much more clear-headed and calm and in good shape to do Step 3.

(I explained to Thomas that when I was writing my dissertation many years ago, I would go for a run. I lived near a park where I had a six-mile and a ten-mile course. I ran one or the other course each day, and ran the longer course when I was really stuck on a problem area of my dissertation. Running was a lifesaver to me. Unsurprisingly, Thomas took up long-distance running during fourth-year theology.)

3. Thomas' third step was to role-play with a mentor or peer to practice the conversation he needed to have with the instructor.

    Asking for help *merely getting started* may be one of the most difficult things to do because it's embarrassing. After all, none of Thomas' peers needed that kind of help. But after the first two steps—seeing the problem concretely and working off his frustration—he was ready to practice what to say to his instructor, and the best way to say it.

4. Step 4: Go to the instructor and ask for help on how to begin.

    Once someone showed him where to start, Thomas could finesse a complicated project through to the end in minute detail and with great proficiency.

Thomas has proved to be a brilliant homilist. He integrates and makes such clear sense of scripture that his homilies are exceptionally organized. He presents them fluidly, without notes. People who knew him as a pre-theologian and now listen to his homilies as a young priest shake their heads in amazement.

SUMMARY

Chapter 5: Communication and boundaries

- Men with autism may have deficits in various areas of communication and awareness of boundaries. These areas may include:

    - Not understanding polite verbal cues, body language, facial expressions, or nuances of tone

    - Being literal-minded

    - Being gullible and socially naïve

    - Not knowing how to make small talk

- - Not being aware of physical or communication boundaries; in particular, with women
  - Not knowing how to ask for help
- Mentoring, including role-play and practice, will be the key to helping seminarians who have problems in these areas.

6. Depression and anxiety

At some point—perhaps as a child, perhaps not until adulthood—many people with autism will recognize that they are not the same, in some ways, as their peers. The differences may reveal themselves in terms of physical coordination, school performance, social relationships, or some other aspect of life.

A man with autism has likely been bullied for much of his life because of his differences and his lack of adeptness at the more subtle aspects of socialization. As a result, anxiety and depression are common among teens and young adults with autism.

In 2013, Jessica Bleil and colleagues and I reported: "Children with ASD are more likely to have difficulties coping with verbal assaults and demeaning statements made by adults because of their limited social knowledge and problem-solving abilities. They also may not have protective factors such as other supportive interpersonal relationships due to their social deficits. As a result, they may resort to a state of learned helplessness or develop a low sense of self-worth and associated depression." ("Maltreatment and Depression in Adolescent Sexual Offenders with an Autism Spectrum Disorder." Bleil, Jessica et al., *Journal of Child Sexual Abuse*, 22: 72-89, 2013.)

Rarely does a person with autism enter adulthood without issues of depression, anxiety, or even trauma. Perhaps more so than others, a man with a higher-functioning form of autism recognizes that he is different from his peers in some ways, but because of his disorder he doesn't know how to correct the problems—or even articulate the problems clearly enough to seek help. Further, he is likely to be hypersensitive to subtle forms of peer bullying, including office teasing. He may feel as if he's being bullied even when a friend might just be gently teasing him. This hypersensitivity puts him on guard as a form of self-protection, preventing him from trusting others or even trusting his own judgment. As a result, his self-esteem is often low and he has only a few interests, which are often solitary by nature.

Recognizing depression and anxiety in a young adult with higher-functioning forms of autism is much more difficult than it is with other adults. Diagnosing it requires a clinician who knows how to ask pointed, specific questions about changes in habits: eating, sleeping, recreation, bathing, and interests. The person with autism will respond to questions readily and literally but may be unable to simply volunteer information that would help with a diagnosis, no matter how badly he wants to be diagnosed and helped. He doesn't have any insight into what you need to know, but he will generally answer your questions as precisely as he can, with the hope that you can help him. The answers to clinical questions, supplemented with standardized depression and anxiety inventories, are often the only way for a clinician to develop a clear, accurate picture of a mood disorder and recommend the correct treatment or therapy.

George

I evaluated George, age fifty-four, while he was in a local jail and had been there for six months. It was a general, routine evaluation of a man who was "benign" on his unit, showing little affect, speaking only when called upon, staying by himself, and not involved in any activities. George was a large man, tall and heavy. He greeted me briefly and responded to my questions with short answers. Overall, he appeared fully oriented, knew why he was in jail, and expressed little emotion about the confinement.

As I began to conclude the evaluation, I asked George, by way of conversation, "How's the food here?" "It's awful," he said. "I've lost thirty-five pounds." I immediately stopped wrapping things up, realizing that I had been fooled by his appearance and his earlier responses. I asked him how long it took him to fall asleep at night and he said it took a long time. I asked if he woke during the night and he said, "How can I sleep with people coming in to check on me all night?" At the time, I didn't have his developmental history, so I administered the Autism Diagnostic Observation Schedule (ADOS) and a depression inventory. The scores showed that George was moderately to severely clinically depressed and also that he was in the high-functioning range of autism.

What I learned first-hand from George was that common vegetative signs of depression may not be as obvious in someone with autism as they would in someone without autism. Even a skilled clinician needs to ask specific questions intended to reveal these signs before ruling out depression. This is especially true when the clinician doesn't know the individual very well or at all. Someone with a higher-functioning form of autism has had years of practice imitating his peers' neurotypical behavior. This makes diagnosing autism alongside affective disorders especially hard, and requires a clinician who has expertise in both.

I have done this type of work for more than twenty years and yet I nearly missed George's autism and his moderate-to-severe depression.

Once I identified depression, George was seen by a psychiatrist who also understood autism. The psychiatrist treated George's depression, which also improved his sleep and appetite.

Anxiety

In the seminary, anxiety can be even more overwhelming than in college. Tests, papers, assignments, mandatory participation in community prayer times, preaching in front of one's peers, high expectations from the rector or abbot or bishop, self-doubt, loneliness, and sometimes homesickness: each of these can cause anxiety, and together they sometimes become more than a man can handle on his own.

During my first semester working at the seminary, most of the men who did *not* have autism didn't come to me. Their thinking seemed to be, "If I talk with the shrink, I'll get kicked out of the seminary." (Fortunately, many of those men slowly began to trust me and eventually some did come to me.) However, the men *with* autism started bringing me their problems and concerns almost immediately.

That was wonderful—except that they all appeared to expect immediate solutions to all their problems. I taught them a treatment paradigm where we prioritized problems and then addressed one or two at a time. The men learned to manage their depression and anxiety, and we worked with a local psychiatrist to obtain medication when necessary.

SUMMARY

Chapter 6: Depression and anxiety

- Most seminarians with autism may also have mood-related issues such as depression or anxiety stemming from bullying or teasing, from the realization that other people see them as different, and from the stresses of being in seminary.

- If these issues are addressed early and straightforwardly by a clinician who understands autism, the depression and anxiety are typically manageable.

7. Rigid behaviors, stimming, and sensory sensitivity

People with autism may have some noticeable behaviors. They may insist on following rigid "scripts" and fall apart when the situation doesn't go as planned. They may "stim"—self-stimulate to comfort or soothe themselves—by, for instance, flapping their hands or jumping up and down. And their senses—touch, taste, smell, hearing—may be extremely sensitive, to the point that they feel acute discomfort or even pain. As with almost all autism-related behaviors, these can be modified and managed with intervention and mentoring.

Rigid behaviors

Few people like change that they can't control, but for people with autism, it can be terrifying. To feel as if they have at least *some* control, many follow a predictable routine to the letter.

Sometimes the seminarian with autism has purposefully taught himself these rigid behaviors, but often he performs them unconsciously. When he was a child, predictable things were a comfort in his uncomfortable world. Regularities such as class schedules, school uniforms, school lunch menus, and the predictable responses of those he was closest to were important because they left him free to address the troublesome, less-predictable areas and events of his life. Rigidity became a go-to coping mechanism.

For adults with autism, these behaviors can still ease anxiety about an uncomfortable situation, whether it's meeting new people, being under some sort of pressure, or feeling any strong emotion. Rigidity can make life in general more predictable and less chaotic.

The flip side of this, of course, is that real life is never predictable. Daily problems can't be solved by resorting to rigidity. It may make the person with autism feel better temporarily, but it doesn't solve the underlying problem.

Seminarians with autism will probably become upset when a routine is interrupted or changed—

particularly if there's been no warning of the change. Sometimes the behavior may seem obsessive-compulsive to others. The seminarian may do it to such a degree that it attracts attention to the behavior rather than to what others should be focusing on.

For example, one priest I know, during consecration, made sure, every time, to use an exact amount of wine and water in the chalice. He kept adding small amounts of both until the mixture was "right" from his perspective. Parishioners anticipated this and focused on his unusual actions instead of the liturgy. The priest seemed to be unaware that his behavior—which to him was private—created a regular disturbance and interfered with the solemnity of the Mass.

Habits are part of our personality, and changing can take a long time and is hard work. This is true for everyone, not just for people with autism. If you've ever tried to quit smoking, using social media, or snacking in front of the television, you know this is true. You have these habits because they comfort you—but they can also harm you. There are at least three steps to changing any habit.

- First we need to realize that our habit—our behavior—can be counterproductive.

- Then we need to remain aware of our behavior, when previously we had done it without thinking.

- And finally, we need to identify a replacement behavior, practice the new behavior, and attempt to use it in real situations.

Just like anyone else, a seminarian with autism may need help realizing that a habit or behavior is counterproductive. If it is an automatic behavior, he may also need help learning to remain aware of it. And he will almost certainly need help practicing better responses and acceptable replacement behaviors. The replacement behavior or routine needs to be acceptable to everyone, including the person with autism. With repetitive practice and role-play with a therapist or mentor over a period of days and maybe weeks, the substitute routine should become natural and happen easily.

People with autism can modify their need to complete rigid routines that interfere with their day-to-day functions. Sometimes they can successfully take it upon themselves to model others' behavior, but more often a clinician will need to help them first realize that there is a problem with their behavior and then find an acceptable replacement behavior.

Tim

Tim, a seminarian with autism whom I worked with, was intellectually gifted, a devoted Catholic, and understood Catholic rituals extremely well. He needed to repeat everything said to him in order to process the information by hearing not only the other person but himself say it. He was unaware that his mumbling under his breath was often audible and disruptive to others. For instance, he could often be heard repeating his instructions during the procession toward the altar. (He did this, in part, because he cared deeply about making sure that his actions were perfect during important liturgical rituals and events.)

Unfortunately, another autism symptom he had was that he expected other people to conform to his rigid behavioral "script." The problem came to a head during a major ceremony involving his bishop. The bishop—a very pastoral cleric—proceeded down the main aisle of the church but deviated slightly from Tim's "script" by stopping briefly to talk with and bless some parishioners near the aisle. Tim quickly became upset by this "deviation," and people heard him mumble a disparaging remark about his bishop. Without prior warning, slight changes to procedures or routines—even *good and pastoral* changes—can make some people with autism uncomfortable.

I'm sad to say that Tim's anger was deep and complex. He said to me once, "Deacon, you know I have autism *and* an anger problem." He was correct. His autism was being addressed well, but his impulse control and anger issues required additional intensive, focused work.

Stimming

"Stimming" is short for "self-stimulation." A stim is a physical behavior indicating a strong emotion —such as love, hate, fear, anxiety, stress, frustration, boredom, or happiness—in someone who doesn't know how to use language to effectively express that emotion. It's a form of communication for those with limited expressive language, but it often has a negative social effect on others. People with autism who are stimming may, for instance, flap their hands, repetitively shake their fingers in front of their eyes, bounce up and down on their toes, rock back and forth, or make various noises.

Self-stimulation prolongs strong feelings. Most of us are inclined to "replay" or mentally relive highly emotional incidents. We revisit that first kiss, a close encounter with death, or an angry conversation. We find pleasure in summoning the same intense emotions we felt at the time of the event—whether those emotions were positive or negative. Almost everyone does this at times, and we're usually able to hide the fact that we're doing it; we keep it inside our heads. People with autism who are stimming, on the other hand, are often unaware that they're doing it and thus don't hide it.

High-functioning adults with autism rarely stim unless there is a significant underlying problem or a sudden overwhelming emotion. As they grow up and learn that unusual behaviors, particularly stimming behaviors, cause others to notice them and may invite bullying, those behaviors often go dormant—although they don't disappear.

When stimming occurs with one of my patients, I will ask a parent when their child did this before, or when they first noticed it. I almost always learn that the stimming began when my patient was a toddler. Stimming behavior tends to be soothing and settling, and small children with autism learn that secret early. When high-functioning adults stim, it's most often in times of extreme stress, grief, sickness—or sleep deprivation. Men studying for the priesthood are often sleep-deprived.

Philip

In my private practice, I re-met Philip and his mother after many years. When I first met him, he was in his upper twenties. I diagnosed him with what was then called Asperger's Syndrome and is now referred to as (High Functioning) Autism, Level 1. Philip was a young executive working competitively without accommodation; no one in his company was aware that he had autism. When I saw him and his mother many years later, she explained that "out of the blue" he had started to "hand flap" again. (As a very young child, he had stimmed by flapping his hands, but he stopped before he entered kindergarten.)

When Philip talked to me all those years later, he was guarded and reserved and did not stim. I asked if anything in their home had changed (he lived with his mother and father), and his mother said that her husband—Philip's father—had just died unexpectedly. That was the key. Philip's world had changed in a huge way, suddenly and for the worse, with the unexpected death of his father. He had no "script" for how to respond or what to do, and his first response was to soothe himself with hand-flapping. His mother and I decided to hold off on any other type of intervention except for supporting him in his loss and explaining to his employer. The hand-flapping faded entirely after two more weeks.

If any type of stimming occurs with a seminarian or a priest, don't react immediately. Find out if he's aware that he's stimming. Ask him what has happened, and give him time to tell you. Depending on the situation, you may want to encourage him to talk to his spiritual and formation directors —and then follow up with him.

Time with his human formator or counselor can play a large part here. Help the seminarian recognize what the behaviors are and when they're likely to happen. Then help him develop his expressive language and possibly find a substitute behavior that is more socially acceptable than stimming.

Sensory sensitivity

Many people with autism have sensory issues that bring about a variety of behaviors. Certain foods or odors may bother or upset them. Certain fabrics, clothing tags, and seams on socks or clothing may irritate them, especially when they're excited or upset. They may be highly sensitive to noise—piercing sounds, or even soft, subtle sounds that no one else notices, such as the buzzing of florescent lights. Even music might bother them; children with autism sometimes instinctively put their fingers into their ears—often at embarrassing times, such as when the soprano solo begins.

As children with autism grow older, they may use noise-quieting headphones in the school cafeteria and even in movie theaters. This makes sense in terms of blocking the ambient audience noises, but your first question may be, "How do they hear the movie?" It actually works; try it for yourself. The audience noises are totally blocked and the movie sound is very quiet. For someone without autism, this will probably be frustrating; movie dialogue and sounds are part of the attraction. For someone with autism, though, who has sensitive hearing, the headphones allow enough movie sounds to make the movie understandable and enjoyable without the risk of loud gunshots, explosions, yelling, a too-loud score, or a theater full of shuffling people and crackling candy wrappers. Some theaters offer special performances, with modified noise levels, for those who have sensitive hearing.

Incense may also be a problem at times. Seminarians need to know which liturgical functions require incense—and what is the smallest amount of incense they can use when it's required. I have worked with seminarians who have pushed themselves through liturgical functions where large amounts of incense were used in a confined area. Even some of the men who were *not* autistic had severe reactions, including incapacitating headaches, but would never ask for medical relief for future functions. (In the same vein, I learned from a fourth-year theologian that he had celiac disease and was allergic to wheat. When I reminded him that we had low-gluten hosts and asked him why he never told the rector, he said that he "didn't want to be a bother." I thought to myself, "A bother? You could have been a role model for others with similar problems where the Church had existing remedies.")

SUMMARY

Chapter 7: Rigid behaviors, stimming, and sensory sensitivity

- Rigid behaviors give a feeling of control and alleviate stress and anxiety. They are usually performed unconsciously and automatically.

- Stimming is physical self-stimulation brought on by overwhelming emotion, when expressive language is inadequate to convey the emotion.

- As is the case with any unconscious behavior, changing these behaviors can be difficult but is possible. It will require a counselor who understands how to develop an acceptable replacement behavior.

- Many people with autism have sensory sensitivity to foods, smells, sounds, or items of clothing. A counselor working with the seminarian can teach him how to ask for help in managing these sensitivities.

8. Welcoming new seminarians (some of whom may have autism)

A new seminarian is a new seminarian. Most of the men entering the seminary will not have a diagnosis of autism. Of those whom I referenced in this book, only two entered the seminary with that diagnosis. The others either didn't disclose their diagnosis or were simply not aware that they had autism. (Most adults today with higher-functioning autism were not diagnosed as children.) Upon entering the seminary, men with autism have needs similar to those without autism. Here are my recommended actions for mentors or upperclass theologians, instructors, human formators and spiritual directors, psychologists, and the rector's council or faculty assembly.

Assign an upperclassman as mentor

Each newly arriving man should be assigned an upperclass theologian to be his mentor. The mentor should be well oriented to that seminary's processes. His assignment should be to:

- explain the basic practices and routines of the seminary, liturgy and prayer schedules, etc.

- help the new seminarian set up his room, and strongly encourage him to use calendars (see Chapter 4).

- clearly communicate policies regarding alcohol, guests, noise, etc., and then provide a clean, typed, paper copy of the policies to the seminarian.

- clearly explain the "gray areas" where rules are not rigid. For example, which articles of clothing—cassocks? clerical shirts?—are mandatory, and when? Which decisions are the seminarian's choice? What do most seminarians choose to do in those situations?

Instructors

To help the new seminarian transition into classwork more easily, each of his instructors should provide a copy of the class syllabus, in writing and in advance. Give it to the seminarian when he arrives on campus. If a new seminarian is identified upon arrival as having autism, he should visit each of his classrooms and meet each instructor before classes actually begin. Because small talk is often difficult for many people with autism, the seminarian may want to simply ask a few questions about the syllabus. This will give him an idea of how the instructor speaks and presents material.

In an ideal world, *all* new students—with and without autism—would follow this practice, but that may not be practical in larger seminaries.

Human formator and spiritual director

As soon as possible, the new student should meet with his human formator and his spiritual director. This is especially important for the seminarian with autism. It will take time for him to know and trust the formator and the director, and they are both critical to his overall priestly formation.

Rector's council or faculty assembly

At the start of each new semester, the rector's council meets and reviews new seminarians. If a new seminarian is already identified as having autism, it will be important for someone who knows the new man—the psychologist, if possible—to provide details that include areas in which the new man will have needs.

Use this same process for the faculty assembly, which also meets early each semester.

In most seminaries, both the rector's council and the faculty assembly meet regularly: typically, once or twice a month. They should receive regular updates on the seminarians with autism as well as those with other disorders or disabilities.

Clinical psychologist

Seminarians with autism, even if they're doing well in most respects, will probably benefit from at least biweekly visits with the seminary psychologist or therapist who has experience working with adults on the autism spectrum. The ultimate goal is a happy ordained priest; meaningful counseling throughout formation may help that happen.

Support during pastoral placements early in formation

Many seminarians receive pastoral placements to local hospitals, nursing homes, and schools, often beginning in their first year of formation. It's important to provide clear structure and direction to all seminarians, but especially to seminarians with autism, who often have difficulty with abstract information or with the lack of an action plan. Knowing clearly what to do, where to go, and whom to report to—along with names and phone numbers—is critical.

9. Pastoral year, transitional diaconate, and priesthood

Ideally, seminarians with autism who are advanced in their formation will have had at least four to six years of excellent support. They will have learned how to manage their autism and will also have learned where they excel. Just as with any other seminarian, they will still need understanding and support from the seminary as they enter into the final phases of formation.

Pastoral year

Some dioceses in the United States require seminarians to take a pastoral year before ordination to the transitional diaconate. During this pastoral year, routines may be less fixed or structured. In addition, the pastoral year starts in the summer, nonacademic part of the year, which may be even less structured than the rest of the year.

Being assigned to a good mentor priest during this time is essential for a seminarian with autism. He's in an unfamiliar setting, under a new priest, working with well-meaning but unfamiliar new staff. He'll have new routines within a different daily and weekly structure. He'll be attending Mass surrounded by hundreds or thousands of people he doesn't know—and they will know *him* by name. All of this may make a seminarian want to panic.

From the very first day, the new pastor—the new mentor—will need to give the seminarian with autism a clear road map of what to do. From the start of the pastoral year, the pastor should review and edit the schedule side-by-side with the seminarian. Each week or month they'll need to create a new schedule for that time period. Eventually a routine will develop. The natural gifts of the seminarian will emerge, and he'll become an active member of the parish.

Transitional diaconate

After returning to the major seminary after the pastoral year, the seminarian will be ordained as a transitional deacon. He will have myriad questions and responsibilities. Learning them and keeping them straight will be his primary need, and where he will need the most help. He will also now preach each week in a parish, and may require help maintaining his confidence and managing a more complicated schedule. All of these issues mean that there should be periodic meetings of several key people: the priest he's serving under, his human formator, his spiritual director, and a psychologist. The purpose of the meetings is to discuss the seminarian's progress and areas of difficulty, and whether he is getting the help he needs.

Ordained priesthood

The hard work continues. It's impossible to predict who will come to the rectory door, and the new priest with autism must have numerous scripts available to him to know how to respond and react. (No new priest, with or without autism, is prepared to handle *everything* he might face.)

A new priest with autism will benefit greatly from a good counselor. If the new priest has a parish of his own and is not working under a pastor, it might also be beneficial for him to have a temporary advisor or temporary mentor. If possible, he should have contact with a group of fellow priests; if some of them are men he knew in seminary and has shared experiences with, that would be best.

The new priest may, especially in the beginning, have a variety of ideas for reading, learning, or growth in holiness or practical skills. His pastor may not always know how to respond to him. I get calls from pastors who don't know what to say or how to respond to a new priest with autism—and it seems that they call me only after a problem has reached critical mass. The new priest should not have to go it alone. He needs to be paired with a pastor who is patient and "gets" autism, or is at least informed and accepting about the disorder and happy to work with the new priest.

Temporary transitional mentoring (after Ordination)

After ordination, the man's pastor is usually his mentor. However, it might be helpful to everyone for the ordinary or abbot to assign a *temporary transitional mentor* to the newly ordained priest for several months, and also when special situations arise. A mentor who does not live with the newly ordained priest is often more able to see the big picture and to help change occur with only minimal disruption to existing routines. Using a mentor priest in this way helps the ordinary or abbot, the pastor, and the new priest.

New-priest peer support group

Newly ordained priests will benefit from joining a small monthly or bimonthly support group of their priest peers that offers a safe place to ask questions, discuss answers, and practice new skills.

10. In closing

God calls us all to live lives of holiness, in spite of our imperfections. Some of us are called to the priesthood or the diaconate. Ordinaries and abbots protectively foster every seminarian to help each one mature and grow in holiness regardless of the hardships, obstacles, disabilities, or bad habits he may be dealing with.

The world desperately needs good priests—as many as we can find, encourage, and shape. Men with an autism spectrum disorder are every bit as likely to become good priests as their seminary classmates are. They're high-functioning, intelligent, and motivated to serve. Many of them have important areas of near-genius that remain to be discovered and developed.

No personality trait or physical disability necessarily keeps a man from being a good priest. Neither do developmental issues, at the high-functioning level. Everything depends on the man's willingness to learn how to manage his issues, and the seminary's support of his efforts to do so. What seminarian—with or without autism—doesn't have at least one behavior that needs to change? And how many seminarians can do that without support?

Like everyone else, seminarians and priests with autism have natural gifts. They also have gifts they've acquired as a result of living with autism. If they feel called to share their gifts as a priest, and if they have understanding and support from the Church, they can become good, dependable, happy priests, serving God and His people for a lifetime.

This book has been a long time coming. When I began working at the seminary, I didn't expect to find any adults with autism as students or coworkers—yet there were many. It's a privilege to work with people who have this developmental disorder. They often see the world in a more honest and genuine way than anyone I know. Yet because of the biases and preconceptions associated with autism, many are not given the opportunity to speak for themselves or to use the gifts that God has given them. I am grateful to the clergy and faculty at St. Vincent Seminary for their willingness to offer seminary formation to men with autism.

I'm also grateful that my publisher and editor believed that men with a developmental disorder could become priests and that this book fills a need.

Autism is one of the most misunderstood, complicated disorders I have ever worked with. I dedicate this book to the men (and women) I've done my best to help over the years, and especially the years I have spent at St. Vincent Seminary. May others experience less of a struggle as they answer God's call to holiness.

www.ingramcontent.com/pod-product-compliance
Lightning Source LLC
Chambersburg PA
CBHW022009120526
44592CB00034B/754